Archibald C. Tait

The Word of God and the Ground of Faith

Six Discourses

Archibald C. Tait

The Word of God and the Ground of Faith
Six Discourses

ISBN/EAN: 9783337191047

Printed in Europe, USA, Canada, Australia, Japan

Cover: Foto ©Lupo / pixelio.de

More available books at **www.hansebooks.com**

THE WORD OF GOD

AND

THE GROUND OF FAITH.

SIX DISCOURSES.

BY

ARCHIBALD CAMPBELL,

LORD BISHOP OF LONDON.

LONDON:
JOHN MURRAY, ALBEMARLE STREET.
1863.

PREFACE.

THE following pages have been written not without reference to present controversies, though I have endeavoured to make them as little as possible controversial. They are published in the hope that they may be of use to some, who, on the one hand, are unable to regard free inquiry respecting the Books of the Bible as a sin, and yet, on the other, desire to retain the deepest reverence for these lively oracles of God. As the discourses were not all preached to the same congregation, it was necessary in the delivery of some of them to introduce passages which were repetitions of what had been before enforced. The endeavour to omit such passages in preparing the work for the press has given it somewhat of a fragmentary character.

FULHAM PALACE,
   23d *June*, 1863.

CONTENTS.

I.
THE GROUND OF FAITH 1
                  PAGE

II.
BIBLE INSPIRATION 18

III.
THE WORD OF GOD IN THE GOSPELS 41

IV.
UNITY OF THE BIBLE 49

V.
THE HISTORICAL BOOKS 62

VI.
THE BIBLE INFLUENCING THE CHRISTIAN LIFE 73

SIX DISCOURSES.

I.

THE GROUND OF FAITH.

[Preached in the Temple Church.]

1 PETER III. 15.

Sanctify the Lord God in your hearts; and be ready always to give an answer to every man that asketh you a reason of the hope that is in you with meekness and fear.

THREE questions, intimately connected, but yet distinct in themselves, are often confounded. 1st. How did I come to hold my religious belief? 2d. What good arguments can I allege in its defence to answer an antagonist who would rob me of it? 3d. When I take myself quietly and thoughtfully to task, what is the real ground on which my soul rests, as assuring me that my belief is right?

The first is a mere question of fact as to my history, the growth of my convictions, and the circumstances which led me to adopt them. The second is a question of logic. The third alone penetrates to the depths of the spiritual life.

It may be that most men adopt their opinions, at first, on what, logically considered, are somewhat insufficient grounds. It does not follow that they are not able vigorously to defend these opinions with sound arguments when once adopted: still less, that a growing experience may not convince them, more and more, day by day, that, however carelessly assumed at first, their faith does, indeed, contain the very essence of that heavenly truth by which the soul's life is nurtured. The first question asks, "How, as a matter of fact, did I enter within the fortress in which I find my safety?" The second, "How shall I repel those who would dislodge me from it?" The third, "What are the advantages it secures for me—which make me every day thankful that I am in it, most unwilling to trust myself without its walls—which assure me that to be where I am is the greatest of blessings?" Perhaps I entered it at first simply by the advice of others, or I was born in it. Perhaps the gates, and walls, and bulwarks by which it is defended, however beautiful and skilfully constructed, have no charms for me, except on account of their usefulness. Perhaps, what gives me real satisfaction is, that, being where I am, I enjoy life, health, energy, in a secure place, and in a good atmosphere, and see myself protected from a thousand evils to which those who wander in the open country are exposed.

Now I cannot help thinking, that in many of the discussions which have been raised as to the grounds of a Christian's belief in his most holy faith, there has often been confusion from our not keeping these three questions distinct.

At first sight, it would seem to be with the second of these questions that the text is solely or principally concerned. If any one demands a reason for the hope that is in you—a heathen magistrate, in days of persecution, or any unbelieving opponent of Christianity at any time, be ready with your defence of it—ἕτοιμοι ἀεὶ πρὸς ἀπολογίαν—your apology—do not let the good cause suffer either from your ignorance of the proper arguments to allege in answer to such an antagonist, or from the temper in which you allege them. "Be ready always to give an "answer to every one that asketh you a reason "of the hope that is in you with meekness and "fear."

There is good teaching here as to the spirit in which the opponents of our faith are to be met. A man, say, is a heathen, or a heretic. He assails Christianity as altogether untrue, or seeks to rob it of those doctrines which, in our estimate, give it all its power. The cause of God's truth will certainly not be advanced by any arrogance or ill-temper, or any want of charitable consideration in those who seek to answer him. The Christians to whom St. Peter was writing were not likely, it is true, to be persecutors, for persecution is the crime of the strong; when men are weak, and liable themselves to be oppressed, it is wonderful how ready they are to appreciate and maintain the arguments in favour of an unbounded toleration. But though the men addressed could not then be persecutors, they might cherish, and show forth in their weakness, that same spirit which would have made them persecute, if they had gained the upper hand. A martyr may be a persecutor in will, while his want of power makes him to be himself the persecuted: and the cause of Christ and His truth may be wronged by the fault of those who, called to maintain it in weakness, and even to suffer for it, meet their opponents in an angry, self-confident, and therefore unchristian spirit. In all controversies, whether we are on the depressed or the winning side, how good for us is St. Peter's teaching as to the spirit in which to argue—speak with meekness, as men who would win souls in love, and have a reverential fear, lest by any fault of yours you harden instead of convincing, and thus do injury to the sacred cause which God has committed to your weak advocacy. You can only conduct your controversy to a good issue, if you enter on it in the spirit of Christ—"Sanctify the Lord God in your hearts."

The Apostle then, in the text, is rightly understood, both as enjoining that we ought to be ready with sound arguments of evidence wherewith to meet the opponents of Christianity, and also as prescribing the reverent loving temper in which we are to argue.

But though the three questions of which we have spoken are in themselves distinct, and not to be confounded, it is not denied that there is a strong affinity in the subject-matter of the several answers to them. From all of them, approached in that reverent spirit which the text prescribes, we may gather materials capable of being applied in their due order and degree to the strengthening of the evidence for Christianity.

As to the first question—What, as a matter of fact traceable in our individual histories, has caused us to believe in Christ? Truly, any pride which we may be disposed to feel in the independence of our conclusions must receive a rude shock—any lurking thought of our imaginary merit in having chosen the way of truth, while others are sunk in debasing ignorance, must melt away, when the light of our actual history reveals how little part we have ourselves borne in the first rise of those convictions from which our faith and spiritual life has sprung. "Who maketh thee "to differ from another? and what hast thou "that thou didst not receive?"[1] A materialistic philosophy might seek to impress upon us that, since all our vaunted privileges of religion, as of civilization, come to us from without, we are in our faith, and in such good living as flows from it, but the passive subjects of some arbitrary law. But the believer in God takes another view of his dependence on outward circumstances: he regards himself as a child in the hands of a kind father, who has ordered all these circumstances of his being by the decisions of united wisdom and love. He does not profess to penetrate the mystery of his being; he knows not how his own felt free-will is reconcileable with the absolute disposal of his destiny by the Almighty and All-knowing, on whom every moment of his life depends; And in the ordering of the events of even his own being, still more of that of others, he acknowledges that there is much in the whole plan and intention the scope of which he cannot as yet guess at, and on which, therefore, he can pronounce no judgment. If others seem to have been but hardly

---

[1] 1 Cor. iv. 7.

dealt with, he has a confident trust that all will come round at last to justify God's wisdom and love; and a calm impartial reflection on his own state usually leaves him very thankful that to himself at least the all-controlling power has manifested such unmerited love. As he is a believer in God, he knows that in what affects the destiny of souls there is no such thing as accident; and that there can be no immutable laws to control the loving will of the Almighty. When asked, then, how he happens to be a Christian, he at once acknowledges that he owes his faith and all its attendant privileges to the kindness of his Father in heaven. He cannot tell you, press him as you will, why the same Father has been pleased to leave others to be Jews, Mahomedans, or Buddhists. But he can tell you at once that it is most illogical confusion to infer that, therefore, there is no better ground for his Christianity than for other people's heathenism. The question has been, hitherto, how he became a Christian, probably in his unthinking childhood. It is quite another matter to ask, now that he is a man, how he can show that Christianity is God's truth. He does not believe that others, left to be reared in false systems, have, as they grow to the maturity of their moral and intellectual nature, any of those calm rational convictions which his expanding powers of thought and feeling force upon him, proving that the arguments by which the faith in which he was trained meets its assailants do rest on the changeless foundations of eternal truth. He passes, as he grows in wisdom and is built up in faith, from the early question, how he became a Christian, to those other two, how he can answer objections by arguments of sound reason, and what are the priceless blessings which he finds, in his own soul's experience, that the Christian faith secures. He does, indeed, never cease to thank God for making him a Christian at first : the kindly dealings of his Father are a frequent subject of his meditation. My friends, we should have fared very differently had God not caused us to be born in a Christian land— had our parents not sought in infancy to secure by our baptism our admission to the many privileges of Christian influence—had we not been taught, from the very first, to pray to God as our Father—a Father reconciled to us in Jesus Christ. Great, indeed, is the advantage we have enjoyed in our Christian education, whereby the stores of ancient wisdom, hived by saints and sages from generation to generation, have been opened up to us freely as we grew in years; and we have learned, by the teaching with which God has surrounded us, to see new beauties of heavenly truth perpetually unfolding in His

Word. How very different must have been our whole character, if now in our maturity we had been only darkly groping after those truths with which, thank God, we have been in some sort familiar from the first dawn of reason. How good has it been for us that the tender memories of childhood have been for almost all of us enlisted on Christ's side, so that when a man is growing hardened in the rough intercourse of life, and the cares and the pleasures of the world combine to deaden his finer sensibilities, something perhaps carries him back in thought to his fresh early days, and the spring of better feelings is re-opened; and then— when the thought of loved friends, long since lost and mourned, bursts upon the heart with that wonderful power which it never loses—these solemn and tender recollections bring back to very many of us the echo of simple hymns, speaking of the love of Jesus, learned at first in the company of those who have been long with Him, and thus secure for our faith a freshness which it was fast losing. We are wise to trace back in thought the instances of God's goodness whereby He first made us Christians, and led us by the hand as Christians in the path of truth. Such thoughts do us good, soften us, give reality to our belief in Christ, and make us, from the recollection of His love past, more hopeful, and therefore more energetic, for the time to come. It is good for us to ask ourselves the first question, How is it that I am a Christian?

But note this, also, that, even in such recollections of our history past, we gain materials not useless for the second and third questions proposed—arguments to answer adversaries, or grounds on which to build up our own convictions. How many a man has said to himself, "This truth is what my mother taught me: if ever I knew a saint she was one. She had a spiritual insight into that unseen world to which she has long since passed; and if in all teachings of human philosophy we are rightly influenced by the decisions of the wise, shall I not, in spiritual things, be greatly swayed by one who lived a truly spiritual life?" Happy they whose earliest childhood is thus privileged to receive sacred impressions never to be effaced, and thus to lay up in the memory associations in which the ripened judgment recognises the germ of sound arguments in support of Christ's truth.

Here is one of the points, then, in which, as we said, our first becomes intermingled with our second, and also with our third question. I became a Christian, say, at first, through the influence of authority: Authority has made heathens as well as Christians: It is not, of course, therefore to be received as a very strong argument in itself for the truth of the system in which I was reared: But still, the authority of the good and the wise has rightly great force. Each man must be much trusted in his own department, and he who lives a spiritual life, and has thus gained a spiritual insight into the truth of God, may claim great weight for his decisions on things spiritual. Hence wise and holy friends, our elders in age—the great divines of other days, whose spiritual lives were reflected in their earnest defences of the Christian faith and exhortations to Christian holiness—the united Church of Christ, so far as its voice is the aggregate of all this wisdom guided according to Christ's promise by His blessed Spirit: these—these handing down a legacy of Christian doctrine and precept from age to age—have not only formed succeeding generations, and thus historically been the causes of our belief, but have, by their heartfelt maintenance of the doctrines they loved, left behind them a strong argument, from their wisdom, goodness, and spiritual enlightenment, that these doctrines are indeed the truth of God taught to them by God Himself.

Our first question thus incidentally does add evidence to help our second. The authority which made me a Christian is, in its degree, an evidence that Christianity is true. And so with the third: that also is intermingled with the second. What gives me personally my satisfaction in the Gospel of Jesus Christ? I have no taste, perhaps, for the somewhat dry study of the Evidences. I do not like to be perpetually reminded of an adversary who denies the most cherished Christian truths, and whom it is my duty to confute. I may regard the habit of mind which is always busying itself with outward defences, as not congenial to the growth of real vital faith within. I may fear the danger, lest I rob theology of its spiritual life and tenderness by turning it into an intellectual struggle with unbelievers: I may dread the deadening effect of a cold array of syllogisms; or the forensic apparatus for the trial of the witnesses who attest each particular of God's marvellous love in Christ. Or again, reverting to that help which our second question borrowed from the first, I may fear lest my leaning on authority as an argument beget a lazy acquiescence instead of a living faith. While granting that a due regard for authority justly calls me to be reverent and circumspect, and not rashly to pass beyond the old landmarks, and to use carefully any help provided by others to aid me in reaching and holding fast the truth, I may still feel that even children, resting on authority, have the firm basis of their belief in something deeper and surer than authority, and that I am no more a child.

I may, therefore, go on beyond the mere outworks of Christian evidences—I may delight rather to dwell on the full meaning of the truths which I love and by which my soul lives. I may plunge at once into our third question. I feel the Gospel of Jesus Christ dear to my heart because it supplies the most pressing wants of my spiritual nature. The more I strive to live above the world, and to free myself from that thraldom in which the things of sight and sense hold me, the more do I understand that without the Gospel of Christ I can make no progress. I feel that I cannot pass through terrible emergencies without the doctrines which Christ teaches—without the comfort of the presence of Christ. Do I desire to have God brought near to me—not a great Being, the abstraction of the good and powerful, dwelling somewhere at a distance beyond the starry heavens, in a region—if region it can be called—where space and time have their limits— but a present Supporter, Guide, and Friend? I feel that no religion which the world has ever dreamed of, has brought God so near, in so endearing a relation as that in which the Second Person of the Trinity is manifested as Jesus Christ. The more I strive after a spiritual life, the more painfully am I conscious of my weakness: How can I persevere? How can I live without that encouragement which is given to me by the thought that the Eternal Son has made atonement for me, and is ever watching to intercede for my weakness? Does the power of evil habits, enthralling my will, make me at times almost desperate? Then there breathes over me the comfort of Christ's promise of the Holy Spirit ready to loose my bonds and to create me anew to a life of holiness. Indeed we might run through the whole cycle of Christian doctrine: every want of our spiritual nature finds its satisfaction in some article of the faith of Christ. This it is that convinces my own soul daily more and more that, without Christ, I can neither live nor die. I care not now how I came to be a Christian. I may not be able to handle evidences so as to confute gainsayers; but this I know of a certainty, that it is indeed good for me to be united to the Lord I love. This is my own soul's stay; and it comes round in time that by what thus helps myself I may also help others, for, after all, no arguments are more forcibly convincing than those which are based on this strictly internal evidence of a holy faith, and show that every want of human nature finds its satisfaction in Christ, and in Him alone.

Our third question then has involved much; much for my own soul's security, much also to convince others. What is practically the ground of my Christianity? How do I know that it is a good thing to be a Christian? How do I feel convinced that I have not believed a fable? I answer no longer that I am led by the authority of others—my parents, the clergy, learned and good men, the Established Church, the Church Universal—I cannot stake my everlasting happiness on these, though it comforts me to think that they are at hand to be my helps. What is my ground of faith? It is not that I have read Paley and Lardner, and can therefore answer captious objections; though I am glad to have such men's arguments on my side. It is—it must be—that in the depths of my consciousness I have a growing conviction, growing daily as I grow in the spiritual life, that nowhere but in the Gospel can I find what is essential to the soul's perfection, nay, to its well-being. My faith thus becomes, in one sense, its own evidence, and that without a paradox. Life is its own evidence, and so is spiritual life. Here is no undue assumption, no begging of the question. Shall a man believe anything? then must he believe what his being, his thinking, reasoning faculties imply, and not only what from the first they imply in their natural state, untutored; he must believe also what is implied in their due exercise and in the gradually acquired condition of their well-being. A man feels that his soul is in its most perfect, when it is in the most Christian, state. From the consciousness of this springs his highest belief in Christ. Such faith is its own assurance, and yet is it logically secure.

Perhaps, you may say, this is all well for yourself, but it must be powerless for others; you will not persuade a man of the truth of Christ, if he doubts it, by such arguments as these. Perhaps not. Yet I would try; I would pass on to swiftly-coming scenes of death, or other terrible catastrophes, and ask how experience teaches that the soul is supported in these. The easy, self-indulgent sensualist, whose life (whatever be his form of mocking orthodoxy) denies a God of purity near him, interceding for him, drawing him heavenwards, breathing into his soul—does his system of practical atheism avail the soul in time of need? Or, again, the worldly trifler? The conceited shallow infidel? Or, alas, the serious doubt-tossed sceptic? His certainly is the less hopeless lot; wandering, he seeks rest, and God will give it: If he seeks it God will give it—certainly in His own good time. But while he is without it, where is his evidence of truth? These all have nothing to lean on: The

Christian has assured rest, and this rest and satisfaction speaks of truth.

To be in heaven at last in the immediate presence of the Father and of Christ, and to know that the Holy Spirit at last has brought each thought into unison with the good and true and holy—to be in heaven, this will bring the strongest evidence of heaven's realities—and why should we not, while still on earth, ourselves enjoy and hold forth to others the strongest evidence of the realities of heavenly truth of which our earthly existence admits, being so trained and disciplined by our faith in God that our hearts feel His presence and His love, and our spiritual eyes become open to the wonders of His nature, even now? If we see, though it be but through a glass darkly, who shall rob us of the conviction that we do indeed see?

II.

BIBLE INSPIRATION.

[Preached under the Dome of St. Paul's.]

1 Cor. II. 13.

Which things also we speak, not in the words which man's wisdom teacheth, but which the Holy Ghost teacheth.

It is sometimes necessary to enter, even on occasions like the present, on disquisitions more or less argumentative as to doctrine. Particular matters in the system of the Church's teaching come, from one cause or another, to be much debated: the public mind is agitated. Men come to ask one another continually what is the truth on this or that question; and they naturally look to the Church's Ministers to suggest topics for their guidance. Now, such matters in the pulpit ought to be handled with as little mixture as possible of any controversy. They can easily be so handled. As to the bitterness of controversy, that is altogether unbecoming at all times in the ministers of Christ; and when we meet for holy worship, obviously the part of the preacher is to set forth positive truth with a distinct view to edification, and to have as little thought as possible of the antagonism of argument. What I have to advance now on a very old subject can scarcely have any novelty. I desire but to set forth, in case they be forgotten, some old acknowledged truths.

Now, this text comes from a passage which is very important, as illustrating what we ought to believe respecting St. Paul's inspiration. "We speak," he says, "not in the words which man's wisdom teacheth, but which the Holy Ghost teacheth." It will be well to look at the verses preceding this text.

Verse 4. "My speech and my preaching was not with enticing words of man's wisdom, but in demonstration of the Spirit and of power."

Verse 5. "That your faith should not stand in the wisdom of men, but in the power of God."

Verse 7. "We speak the wisdom of God in a mystery, even the hidden wisdom ... which none of the princes of this world knew."

Verse 9. "As it is written, Eye hath not seen, nor ear heard, neither have entered into the heart of man, the things which (*i.e.* in the Gospel) God hath prepared for them that love Him."

Verse 10. "But God hath revealed them unto us by His Spirit."

And again, verse 12. "We have received the Spirit which is of God, that we might know the things that are freely given to us of God."

Thus far the Apostle may be held to be speaking, chiefly at least, of the substance of his teaching. I can scarcely understand how any one making a claim to have received the substance of his teaching from a supernatural and Divine source could assert his claim more explicitly than in such words. In the text however the Apostle goes further. Turning from the substance, he comes even to the form of his teaching, and says, " These things "—viz. the truths before stated to have been revealed—" we speak in the words which the Holy Ghost teacheth."

As to the substance of the Gospel preached by St. Paul and his fellows, if it was not given by revelation from Heaven, they certainly thought it was; and they say that it was, not only here, but in every chapter of their writings. We might well ask, if it did not come by revelation from heaven, whence did it come? It were a strange system for men to spin out of their own heads, or the feelings of their own hearts. But that is not now our point. The Gospel, I say, claims in every page of its records to come from heaven, and that directly, by a supernatural revelation; so that we cannot accept it without this doctrine of its supernatural and miraculous origin as part of it—nay, as connected with its very essence. St. Paul, therefore, and his followers, if the Gospel which they preached and for which, remark, they went through daily sufferings, and were ready to lay down their lives—the Gospel which now for so many centuries has been the source of countless blessings to the human race—if this Gospel, I say, was true, St. Paul and his followers were the ministers of a revelation from heaven. They taught a system which God gave them—which they did not invent for themselves or receive from any other human inventor. The substance, therefore, of the Gospel, if it is true, is miraculously communicated. This is what the Apostle states in the earlier verses of the chapter before us: "These things God hath revealed unto us by his Spirit."

But further, if it be granted that it was heaven-given truth which these teachers were to preach, was it not natural to expect that they should be placed under some heavenly guidance in their preaching, lest God's truth might suffer through the imperfection of the human instrument of its promulgation? If the men whom Christ selected were to have this heavenly treasure in earthen vessels, was it not probable that He would be ready to enable the vessel to do its part well? Was it not to be expected, I say, that He would give them an assurance that the same Spirit which revealed the substance of the Gospel would guide its first teachers—"leading them into all truth"—

"bringing all things to their remembrance" whatsoever He had revealed—and saving them from mistakes in its transmission? Was it not in fact to be expected that the promulgator of a revelation should be an inspired man—inspired, I mean, to teach—guided and secured from all important error in his solemn declarations of the truth—inspired in his first preaching, and if so, surely inspired also in the record he was to leave behind him in writing of what that preaching was? St. Paul, I say, in the text asserts that he was so inspired. "These things we speak in the words" or discourses (at all events in the form) "which the Holy Ghost teacheth." I take St. Paul before us, therefore, to assert in this place that not only does he teach, as the previous verses state, heavenly as opposed to human doctrine, but also that he imparts it in a heavenly form—the same Holy Spirit first giving a knowledge of this truth to the Apostle's own soul, and then guiding him as its promulgator in his endeavours to impart it to others. That there was this heavenly guidance in the mode and form of the Apostle's teaching, I take to be the doctrine that St. Paul—and if St. Paul, so the others—was inspired in his speaking—and if in his speaking, so also surely in his writing.

Of course there is no time here to enter on any very detailed argument in proof of the inspiration of the first preachers of the Gospel. I confine myself to reiterating—

1. That inspiration, in the sense of a supernatural and heavenly guidance, controlling the first announcement and original written record of the Gospel system, seems to follow as a natural consequence from that system being divine. If God gave the knowledge of it in order that that knowledge might be communicated to the world by those who first received it, is it not probable that He would himself superintend that first step of its transmission, without which, however it might bless the hearts of a privileged few, it never could have struggled as He intended into outward public utterance to be the established and sure benefactor of mankind from age to age? In other words, Revelation naturally implies inspired teachers.

2. I reiterate, that our Lord gave to His disciples distinct promises of Spiritual aid, which have a natural fulfilment in such heavenly guidance.

3. That St. Paul, in the text, as elsewhere, asserts that he enjoyed this guidance, urging that not only was the truth he taught truth from heaven, but that he had heavenly help in teaching it.

4. That the written record of the Apostle's teaching is but the crystallized form of his

spoken words. If the man was inspired in his utterances, so is the book which preserves them.

5. That if St. Paul was thus guided, it would be incongruous to suppose that similar help was denied to St. Peter and St. John. All this I have already touched in commenting on the context.

And now I note further—

6. That if the Epistles were thus inspired, we have a strong *à priori* ground to attribute a similar inspiration to all the books of the New Testament. Can we suppose that apostolic men were helped by God in one part of their deliberate and solemn teaching, intended for the guidance of the Church, and not in another? If St. John, for example, as a matter of fact and history can be proved to have written the Revelation, it is ridiculous to suppose that his Epistles were thus inspired and the Revelation was not.

7. Nothing could be so important for the Church as to have a perfectly trustworthy account of the Lord Jesus' life, and death, and teaching. Inspiration guiding St. Paul, that he might accurately communicate the impressions he received from heaven—can we conceive that God granted this without exercising a similar providential guidance over those who were commissioned to hand down to us the actions and sufferings and discourses of Him whose shoc-

latchet St. Paul would not have thought himself worthy to unloose? The Lord of Glory, the Eternal Son, stooping to earth, living and dying for men, as the inspired writers of the Epistles everywhere assert that He did, as the basis of all their systems,—is it conceivable that He could have so come, and that He who inspired the Apostles to preach about Him should not have inspired those who were to leave, for all ages, the written record of that life on which all the Gospel system hangs? And, further, if St. Luke was thus inspired to write his Gospel, we can hardly hold that he was left to himself to grope his way darkly and uncertainly through the history of the Acts.

The inspiration asserted in the text, by natural inference, then, renders probable, if it does not demonstrate, the inspiration of the whole New Testament. This seems the inevitable conclusion of sound logic.

It is sometimes thought that Paley has not been explicit enough in arguing for the inspiration of the books of Scripture; but grant their genuineness and authenticity, in proof of which he so successfully labours, and their inspiration follows.

8. I remark, eighthly, this very significant fact, that the early Christians, being either Jews or so connected with Jews as to understand and adopt

their view of the Scriptures, added on the several books of the New Testament, as they were written or came to light, to the already existing canon of the Old. Now we know the view which the Jews took of the Old Scriptures. From tradition, or Church authority, or good historical evidence, or from the internal light of that heavenly majesty of truth which breathes about them, on whatever grounds (whether they were good or bad has nothing to do with our present argument), the Jews did look upon the Old Testament as the inspired word of God. When, therefore, we find those Jews, who became Christians, and their fellow-converts, consenting to place the works of their contemporaries in the same category as these old Scriptures, what are we to infer? They found men, who were either still living or very recently dead, claiming to be inspired, as they believed the old prophets were; and they allowed their claim, and placed their writings side by side with those of the old prophets. Is it conceivable that, as Jews, they could have done so without sifting their claims? We are not speaking of uninstructed ignorant men, like those who among ourselves make canonical Scripture of the Book of Mormon: we know who the early Christian writers were, and what they were. Is it conceivable that, living in days when the Apostles were scarcely gone to their rest, they would have allowed their claims without having sifted them? Would any one of such men, suppose in our days, and holding our ordinary views as to the inspiration of the Bible, allow any modern book, say one of the last century, to be added to the Bible because its writer claimed to be inspired, unless some surprising proof were at hand to show that he was really what he professed to be?

I note, then, that the writings of St. Paul and the other New Testament books, being thus placed in the same category as the Old Testament, not when they came down from hoar antiquity, but so soon after they were written, must be taken as a proof that men who had the means of sifting the facts saw no incongruity in allowing that the writers of these books were really messengers from God, as they believed the Old Testament prophets had been in remote ages.

And, having thus strengthened the claims of the New Testament, by its being set side by side with the Old, I see no inconsistency in calling attention, in the ninth place, to this fact:—

9. That still for us, now-a-days, the authority of the Old Testament rests on the New. It might be otherwise with the Jews, in our Lord's time; though doubtless, as follows from what we have first said, it must have been a great confirmation to their faith in the claims of the

prophets and seers of the old dispensation to have the opportunity of testing, and to be forced to acknowledge the similar claims advanced by apostles and evangelists so near their own day. No doubt, when once they accepted Christianity, they found in the Gospel, with the tested record of all its miraculous manifestations, a stronger ground than they had ever known before for believing that God, at sundry times, and in divers manners, spake in times past unto their fathers by the old prophets. But, however it was with them, certainly with us, now eighteen hundred years after their day, the strongest proof of the divine authority of the Old Testament is found in the New.

We need not speak of the Lord of Life—himself incarnate truth—paying the homage of omniscience to the ancient Scriptures: Look even to the Apostles. Could any reasonable man suppose that they were commissioned by God to announce a message from heaven which based its teaching on these old Scriptures, and referred to them continually—that their message was heavenly truth, and that they were inspired from heaven as to the mode in which they were to communicate it—and yet maintain that the view of these old Scriptures, which runs all through the message, was absurd and false? If I believe the New Testament, I must acknowledge the Old. The very same book to which Christ and His apostles were for ever appealing, guarded with the most jealous care both by Christians and their enemies, this very same book is in our hands now. I must acknowledge it to be what Christ and His apostles say continually that it is.

Once more, then, to recapitulate:

It was natural to expect that the writers of the New Testament should be inspired. Our Lord promised them inspiration. They themselves claim it; and in other matters they speak nothing but the simplest truth. The claims of all of them hang together; so that if one was inspired, it is natural to conclude so were all. As a matter of history, the men who lived nearest to their times, and had the best means of judging, believed them to be inspired. If they were inspired, and the New Testament is the Word of God, so also is the Old.

Here is a series of dry logical arguments by which to meet objections.

Consider, now, this phrase: The Word of God —God's Word, written in the sacred books and preached by their authors. How much is implied in this phrase—The Word of God? This at least, that we are to listen to it, to read it, to discuss it, with the deepest reverence. As Moses of old, feeling that we stand on holy ground: God called to Moses, and said, "I am the God of thy father, the God of Abraham, the God of Isaac, and the God of Jacob."[1] No wonder that he hid his face in reverence. He knew the voice when it spake to him, and bowed before his Maker. As Abraham[2] fell on his face when God talked with him. As Job,[3] when the Lord spake to him out of the whirlwind, abhorred himself, and repented in dust and ashes. As Elijah[4] at Horeb, wrapped his face in his mantle, that he might listen to the easily recognised accents of the still small voice. My friends, it is indeed something for a human being to hear the Word of God.

The Word of God written—this is what we have in our hands—manifested to be indeed the Word of God by what it has done in the history of human souls—now, for how many centuries—thus manifested more convincingly than even by the strict logical arguments we have adduced, to be in very truth what it professes to be, a message, or a series of messages from the Lord of all souls—that, whereby God speaks to his creature man—God's message in its substance, and his message also in its form—not losing aught either of its heavenly substance or its heavenly form, on account of the imperfection of the human instruments through which it has been transmitted.

[1] Exod. iii. 6.   [2] Gen. xvii. 3.   [3] Job xlii. 6.   [4] 1 Kings xix. 13.

I do not wish to enter here on any intricate or subtle questions as to all that inspiration implies, or how far it is either possible or expedient to discern those fine limits which mark the convergence and separation of the divine and human elements in the aggregate written word. The human characters of the writers of the several portions of Scripture, the transitory circumstances by which they were surrounded when they wrote, the human helps which aided them, and the matters of secondary and mere human interest of which they incidentally treat in delivering their great message of that truth which concerns the salvation of the soul,—all these things may properly be examined in their due place by a reverent and religious criticism. And it will argue a want of faith if we are continually taking alarm as if the Gospel of the Lord Jesus Christ was endangered, whensoever these subjects are treated of.

But what I plead for is this: that the presence of the Divine element be never forgotten in our speculations as to the human; and that the thought of this Divine presence shall solemnize the critic's mind, and regulate his every sentence. I claim that God's Word written be treated by good men as they would, in old days, have treated his Word spoken. If it had been our privilege to hear St. Paul preach, or to listen to the outpourings of the prophetic spirit of Isaiah; while the Apostle or the seer urged us, in God's name, to repentance and to holiness— would any man amongst us, of religious mind, have been splitting straws to ascertain the exact limits according to which the inspiration moulded the natural and human eloquence, which was the vehicle of its communication? Take the case of uninspired men who speak with authority: a reverent spirit will ever make us very cautious how we try to distinguish, in the teachings, say of a wise and good parent, how far we may distrust or undervalue any one particular portion of the lesson of truth and holiness which the whole tenour of his life urges on us. And had we been of the number who clustered round the Lord of Life, say, on the hill-side, when he spake the Sermon on the Mount—what estimate should we have formed of any one of our fellow-hearers, who, instead of gladly listening to the whole heavenly lesson, busied himself in carping at words and phrases, and in trying to separate them into two classes, and referring one to the divine, and the other to the human Christ? My friends, this is not the spirit in which we listen, hoping to be taught of God.

Acknowledging then the Bible to be the Word of God, we listen to it all with reverence. But for our satisfaction and the surer confirmation of our faith, lest any should suppose that we are losing ourselves in the vagueness of a general statement, note in conclusion that, when we say generally the Bible is the Word of God, we recognise many distinct propositions.

1. Spoken words recorded—*i.e.* faithfully recorded, are still, long ages after they were spoken, real and living words. And words have their value as the true expression of the feelings of the heart, and actions are even a more deliberate expression of such convictions, being in fact words and feelings deliberately manifested and attested in outward deed. It follows that in a good biography we have the true utterances of him, the story of whose life it tells. The recorded discourses then of the Lord Jesus, and His short pregnant sayings, and the teachings of His heavenly life, set forth in the simple narrative or appended to it and amplified by His chosen servants filled with the Holy Ghost, these all speak to us as His voice from Heaven —a voice searching the conscience—rousing the slumbering soul; that very voice, indeed, of the Son of Man, which at last the dead shall hear in their graves, and they that hear shall live.

2. And as with this recorded direct teaching of the Lord Jesus, so with those overflowings of Heavenly wisdom which He (the source of

light and truth and knowledge) gave forth through the faithful and truthful spirits of St. Paul, St. Peter, St. James, and St. John, and all their noble company. They also being dead yet speak; and they speak by delegated authority from Him who lives ever.

3. And then, in the old books to which they and He are for ever pointing as the Word of God—prophecy as set forth in these books— that is, not the foretelling of coming events only, but the whole of the prophets' teaching, as revealing, warning, guiding—prophecy "came "not in old time by the will of man, but holy "men of God spake as they were moved by the "Holy Ghost." In the long roll, then, of more than a thousand years of prophecy, stretching from the sojourn in Egypt to the return from the Captivity, we as truly as the two disciples journeying to Emmaus (and, thank God, under the same guidance as they) are privileged to recognise God's voice, as they recognised it, when the Lord Jesus, beginning at Moses and all the prophets, expounded unto them in all the Scriptures the things concerning Himself.[1] May we listen as they did. Their hearts burned within them, while He talked with them, and opened to them the Old Testament Scriptures.

[1] Luke xxiv. 27.

4. But, in the Bible, we have not only the Biography of the Son of Man, and of God's chosen servants and their prophetic utterances: we have also, in the Old Testament as well as in the New, a record of the doings of God himself—God shown in other manifestations before He came to dwell among us in Jesus, the Son of Man. It is trite to observe that, while all ordinary records give but the human side of the world's history, the Bible gives the divine. The whole of the Bible history then, as well as its biography strictly so called, and its prophecy, is the word of God. It tells us, sometimes in the plain matter-of-fact manner of modern annals, sometimes in the dark poetic form in which all history veils itself in what we call pre-historic times—how, if we may say so, God has felt towards man—how He has dealt with him—how He has controlled his destiny, and made him serve His will, ever yearning over him with a Father's love—how He weaned him gradually from a low morality and debased religion into which he had sunk, giving him higher and brighter truth as he was able to bear it, and training him in a better polity, with laws enforced on higher sanctions than the world's legislators could devise—thus preparing him, step by step, for the revelation of the great Christian polity in Jesus Christ.

5. But besides what we thus recognise of the utterances of the Divine Voice, inherent in the book now, as it was of old in heaven-appointed speakers, note that there is also the same Voice speaking still within the heart and understanding, and reason and conscience of him who rightly reads or hears. "The Word of God is quick:"[1] (or, as we may render it) Living is the Word of God—not surely here merely the written record, nor even the spoken voice, but He who is manifested in both. Living is the Word of God, and "powerful, and sharper than any "two-edged sword, and piercing even to the di-"viding asunder of soul and spirit, and of the "joints and marrow, and is a discerner of the "thoughts and intents of the heart." As of old, many who heard Christ, hearing, heard not,[2] for their heart was waxed gross and their ears were dull of hearing till the Living Word, which spake in vain without them, came within them and quickened them to listen, to apprehend, to understand, and, in the highest sense, to know the truth, so is it still. Christ's promises of the guiding Spirit are not to be limited to the first preachers and writers of His Gospel; though we have seen they justly appropriated these promises as guaranteeing to them a higher guidance than we dare aspire to. Still for us also, in our

[1] Heb iv. 12.   [2] Matt. xiii. 13.

degree, these promises stand sure. " Behold, I am with you alway, even unto the end of the world." To the Christian conscience, then, enlightened by the Holy Ghost, the Word of God speaks within, and God Himself thus helps us to unlock the treasures of His written Word without. The real author of the Sacred Books is living still, and speaking to His people's hearts. No fear for those who humbly place themselves under His divine guidance, lest they fail to learn such lessons from the Bible as will save their own souls. No fear but the more they grow under His divine teaching, using reverently all human helps as in His sight, the more wise will they become to discover for themselves and unfold to others the unsearchable riches of Christ. A humble-minded Christian, in interpreting Scripture, as he uses all other subordinate helps, certainly calls to his aid the recorded decisions of the wise and good, and of the collective Church. But it is his comfort to know that he has himself as direct access as any, who have gone before him since the Apostles' days, to the distinct help of God.

Under this guidance, the enlightened Christian reason and conscience will find no practical difficulty in distinguishing in the history between those actions and words which are recorded for our imitation, and those on which either no judgment is passed, or which are distinctly written for our warning. Again, under this same teaching, as we follow the stream of Scripture, and see how God's revelation, age after age, sweeps onward in its fertilizing course, spreading gradually, as it advances, a purer knowledge and a higher civilization, we shall find no difficulty in noting the steps by which a more evangelical morality and a higher spiritual religion exalts and purifies the lower teaching of the law and of the older covenant. As in reading God's commandments we can easily distinguish—as indeed we do every day—between the passing letter and the ever-binding spirit, so let me point it out distinctly—for men's minds are agitated in this matter by some groundless fears—if thus taught of the Living Word within, we shall find no practical difficulty of any real moment in distinguishing (where it is requisite), in the other portions also of the Bible, between the substance of the Divine teaching and its mere accidents—between the heavenly lessons which God intended to communicate, and the mere imagery with which He surrounded them. Neither shall we find any practical difficulty in the fact that, while certainly the Bible does continually, as it were, impinge on questions of geology, and astronomy, and ethnology, and on intricate calculations of family or national genealogy, still no human being can tell exactly how far the sacred writers had any guidance in such matters, or were left by God entirely to themselves.

Certainly such matters concern but the outer case, and scarcely touch that inner treasury of those great religious truths which God ordained the Bible to guard, that through them He might instruct, train, and save men's souls.

This sketch of these few imperfect thoughts on a great subject may prove not useless in days of hazardous controversy. To sum up all and close: The Church Universal throughout the world—all tribes and sects and denominations of men, who have ever called themselves Christians —have in all ages acknowledged that the Bible is the Word of God. Our own Church, beyond others, in its doctrinal statements and the daily practice of its worship and its teaching, proclaims for ever how precious is this truth. The better, and holier, and wiser men have become in past days, the more have they intelligently prized the Bible. The Bible is the Word of God; in itself outwardly and objectively for all, whether they will hear or whether they will forbear; but in an especial sense it is the living Word subjectively for faithful souls taught of God. The eternal Father speaks in it directly; the Lord Jesus speaks in it directly; The Father, Son, and Holy Spirit speak in it through the teaching of holy men inspired. We catch the accents of the divine voice in their words of heavenly wisdom, in their recorded holy deeds, in all the divine arrangements whereby man was raised, age after age, from the degradation into which the fall had cast him, that he might be ready at last for the complete fulfilment of the promises of salvation in Jesus Christ. In all these ways God speaks to us, and His voice without is re-echoed by the voice within. God grant to us to be in the attitude of prayerful listeners. "Speak, Lord, for Thy servant heareth." *

* 1 Sam. iii. 9.

III.

THE WORD OF GOD IN THE GOSPELS.

[Preached at St. James's, Piccadilly.]

St. John XX. 30, 31.

And many other signs truly did Jesus in the presence of his disciples, which are not written in this book. But these are written that ye might believe that Jesus is the Christ, the Son of God; and that believing ye might have life through his name.

PREACHING lately elsewhere on Bible inspiration, I pointed to many senses in which the Bible is the Word of God. Amongst others I noted that in it we have the utterances partly in His actions and partly in His recorded words, of the Lord Jesus Christ—God incarnate. St. John says in the text respecting his Gospel, that it is a record of such utterances preserved for an especial purpose, viz. to give life to men's souls. "These"— viz. these records in my Gospel—"are written that ye might believe that Jesus is the Christ, and that believing ye might have life through his name."

* * * * *

I adduced certain conclusions, which the statement, that the Bible is the Word of God, does not, and certain others which it does, imply.

It is granted, now, I suppose, by all theologians, that we have no reason to believe God intended the Bible to teach those scientific truths, a knowledge of which is attainable by man, through the use of his own unaided reason. We look with pity on an age which could attempt to stay the progress of astronomical science by imprisoning the astronomer, and which had so little faith in God's Word revealed, as to fear that its heavenly mission might be hindered by too intimate an acquaintance with the secrets of Nature. A man can have no real belief in the trustworthiness of the Bible who is alarmed at every fresh discovery in geology or ethnology, or the records of primitive history. Let him fix in his mind that the Bible has its mission distinct and clear to teach that spiritual truth which breathes life into dead souls; to stir the conscience; to draw it to God in Jesus Christ; and while the man listens to the voice of God thus speaking to him in and through the Bible, all such unbelieving fears will drop from him. Let every scientific student do his work thoroughly and well. The Church of God never suffered yet by the progress of science, and never will. It may be necessary at times to suspend our judgment as to how newly discovered truths can be reconciled with established theories of Bible interpretation; but the divine voice will still sound clear and convincing, and whatever clouds may seem to spread darkness for a time, God will manifest himself at last shining brightly through them all. We cannot determine now how far, as time goes on, it may be necessary for some amongst us to review and modify theories of inspiration which they have received and cling to without sufficient evidence and on grounds of mere human tradition. Indeed, I incline to think it may fairly be doubted how far a very strictly defined theory of inspiration is good in itself, or how far God ever designed that we should form such a theory. There are many subjects on which in the present imperfect state of our information we feel certain that a strictly defined theory must be erroneous; and this holds especially in all those subjects which touch on the mysteries of our own and of God's being. Speaking of the inspiration of the Bible, we have before us a divine and a human element—imperfect human language, employed for a distinct purpose by Him who is All-perfect and divine. I do not feel sure that, however we may speculate, we shall ever be able to mark with great accuracy where the human ends and the divine begins. Providentially, it will very seldom happen that for faithful souls any serious difficulties arise from the want of such accuracy. This book is to us and to the Church of God the guide of life; God designed that it should be so. From beginning to end it is replete with His message. All earnest Christian souls have reverenced the book and delighted in its teaching. It has a fulness, richness, spirituality and power of searching the heart, which speak of its divine author. I know and acknowledge gladly that there are many things which it never was designed to teach me. I know that in many respects God intended it to conform to the language and mode of thought which prevailed when and where its human authors lived. But the great spiritual purpose for which God designed it, the book does and ever will subserve. I may fairly doubt how far I am dealing with it reverently or faithfully if I try to divert it to any other use.

Better, on the whole then, perhaps, to leave theories, and to dwell, one by one, on some of the great truths which the doctrine that the Bible is the Word of God does certainly imply. Of these truths, when speaking elsewhere, I have enumerated many. One is brought before us in the text. The Bible is God's word in this amongst many other senses, viz. that in it we have the record of the utterances, through action and through speech, of God incarnate, the Lord Jesus Christ.

The Church's rule wisely brings Holy Scripture before us, in its completeness, for our daily reading throughout the year. We are not encouraged to draw distinctions as to degrees in the edification to be gained from its several parts. At the same time, it is well that no part is so thoroughly known as the narrative of the Gospels. Children in our schools receive their first lessons from it. We hold it disgraceful in an educated man not to be able to understand the most distant allusion to its history: thank God that we know it so well in its outward details: may He grant us, as we pass from our childhood to old age, to be ever growing in the power of fathoming the depths of its spiritual teaching. Take the book—the short book of which the text states the design. This Gospel of St. John is, in its size, but a pamphlet; yet how has it moulded the religion, the morality, the civilization of the world! How familiar are we with its human author, though he speaks so little of himself! We gather his character from the way in which it glows in the picture he has left us of the Master whom he loved. No wonder that the imagination of so many centuries has grown familiar also with the supposed type of the Saint's outward lineaments, that the mention of his name suggests to us a distinct image of the bright apostle of love. But it is in his subject, not in himself, that he has his lustre and his power. To be the chief Biographer of the

Lord Jesus Christ, to have enjoyed the tenderness of His long intimacy in the days of His flesh, and been privileged afterwards to see Him and hold lengthened intercourse with Him in beatific vision; so that the name of the Apostle is linked with that of his Lord for ever—an enviable lot, truly! The man who was thus privileged, telling us, even with his own human voice, of his human experiences, would be entitled to be listened to as a messenger direct from God. But it is Christ, not St. John, who is the Speaker in this Gospel—Christ, the Eternal Word. My friends, how dully, morning after morning, do we hear these divine discourses and the record of that divine example! What good effect has it on men's minds, amid the pre-occupations of their busy or thoughtless life, to be forced to listen to some words of ancient human wisdom, or dwell on the bright example of some good man of old? In human history and biography, the good of past ages call to us from the distance to withdraw our thoughts from the absorbing present, while, being dead, they thus speak to us. But He who speaks to us in the divine narrative of the Gospels, is not dead now, and is not distant—" I am He " that liveth, and was dead; and, behold, I am " alive for evermore"—as present with us now, while we read His history as He was with St.

John, when He laid His kind hand upon him in the beginning of the vision of the Apocalypse. Such thoughts make the reading of the Bible a distinct devotional act like prayer. If we can realize such thoughts, our Bible readings, like our prayers, bring us into the immediate presence of the Lord who died for us. We are right to study the Gospels with all helps of common human learning, and seek to examine their language and the structure of their sentences grammatically and logically; but if we are devout Christians, and Christ is what we believe Him to be, we cannot read them like any common book; we must approach them reverently and in the spirit of prayer, when we recall that they are written for this express purpose, that we may believe that Jesus our Saviour, made in our likeness as the Son of Man, and dying for us, is Christ our Prophet teaching us—our Priest, who once atoned and now intercedes for us—our King, who ever lives to reign over us and to guide us; and that this record of Christ is given us by God, that, believing, we may have life through His Name. The world would be cold and comfortless, were it not illumined and warmed by the brightness which, through the Bible, is ever beaming from Him who is the Light of the world. Other modes might be thought of, whereby Christ might speak to His people, from age to age. Without the Bible, we might have known something, much or little, of His sayings and example through uncertain tradition, or some common human history; and we need not have been separated from His presence, vouchsafed in His sacraments and in answer to prayer; but still, had the Bible been denied us, the whole aspect of our relations to Him would have been greatly changed, and it is difficult to understand in what other way, without the Bible, we could have been brought so near. The Church Universal, in all ages and countries, in many tongues, has returned thanks to God for this sacred deposit, and has guarded it with jealous care: let us see that we rightly use it, that, believing, we may have life through Christ's Name.

IV.

UNITY OF THE BIBLE.

[Preached at St. James's, Piccadilly.]

REV. XXII. 18, 19.

I testify unto every man that heareth the words of the prophecy of this book, if any man shall add unto these things, God shall add unto him the plagues that are written in this book: and if any man shall take away from the words of the book of this prophecy, God shall take away his part out of the book of life, and out of the holy city, and from the things which are written in this book.

LET it be granted, that this solemn warning applies to the Apocalypse, and in its first intention has no reference to the whole book, the Bible. This granted, we are still bound to consider how far it sets forth a general principle applicable to the Word of God as a whole. In the old days, God had thus fenced the law given to Moses: "Ye shall not add unto the word which I command you, neither shall ye diminish aught from it;"[1] and "What thing soever I command you, observe to do it: thou shalt not add thereto, nor diminish from it."[2] Indeed, the general principle approves itself at once to common sense—not more applicable,

[1] Deut. iv. 12.   [2] Deut. xii. 32.

certainly, to the Apocalypse or the Mosaic Law, than to the Word of God generally. If there be such a thing as a revelation from God to man, obviously man must be very careful of it: he must be jealous in guarding this treasure. As no false jewels must be numbered with the true, so none of the true must be suffered to be abstracted. The lesson thus generalized has two bearings on the controversies of the day. Superstition must not exalt human traditions to the rank of revelation, and the free inquiries of Bible criticism must be anxiously reverent.

Now this double applicability of the words of the text, in their primary particular and secondary general reference, suggests an important matter, to which I wish to bespeak attention. The Bible is a compound of many books, but it is also one book. It is not safe for us in our Bible studies to forget either of these truths. There was a time when we were disposed to regard the Bible too much as one whole—to overlook that vast interval of fifteen hundred years, during which the great revelation of the Gospel in Jesus Christ was, as it were, travailing to the birth; to forget how diverse was the civilization, political condition, moral and religious feeling, of the people to whom God sent His messages, at various epochs in those many centuries; and how diverse, also, were the characters and circumstances of the several human instruments whom He employed at different times to be His messengers. It is folly to interpret poetry and prose—primitive history and contemporary annals—philosophical treatises and Psalms of praise—codes of legislation and sketches of domestic life—by the same stereotyped rules: to suppose that Judea and the Jews were the same in the age of Tiberius, as they were when Joshua first crossed the Jordan with his victorious host; or to read the Bible as if it all had been written in one age and by one man, like the Antiquities of Josephus. Its one Divine Author, controlling all, nowhere supersedes the various human instruments to whom, if we may so speak, he delegated his work.

No doubt then it is quite right that the several books of the Bible should be examined one by one, and that each book or series of books should be treated, so far as may be, as in one sense a whole complete in itself. The chief province of Bible criticism in the present age has been to examine the books thus minutely in detail. But it is well worth considering whether this has not now gone so far as to make it very necessary that the attention of our critics should again be directed steadily to the fact that this book, amid the variety of its parts, is still all of it one great whole. A great historical picture must be very inadequately appreciated by him who is altogether taken up with examining the lineaments of the various figures or the minute drapery of their dress, and does not view the whole group as one. Again, in physical science men become narrow-minded, and take most inadequate views of nature if they have no employment except to pry into minute details in that particular department which most attracts their own taste. The great philosopher is he who can trace the orderly relations of various parts in the one universe. Again, to produce practical results a microscopic division of labour is indeed invaluable: but still all agree that the highest of human employments are those in which the detailed work of labourers in contracted spheres is wielded by some enlarged intelligence for the instruction or guidance of mankind. And so in like manner there can be no high and true criticism of the Bible which does not connect its limited examination of particular fragments of heavenly truth, by turning its reverent gaze on the vast colossal mass which has grown through the accumulated deposit of ages to the proportions of a great mountain, having its base in the deep foundations of the earth, and its summit in heaven.

I heard lately the reflection of a good and holy man, quite awake to every phase of really intelligent criticism, and by no means disposed to reject novelties because they are new: he had lately been following the course of the Bible lessons in the Church's Calendar morning and evening; and he said this thought was forced on him: "How shall I explain the miracle, that I recognise the accents of the same Gospel of life in books whose human authors lived so many ages apart, under such totally different circumstances, except by turning to one great Divine Author who taught and controlled them all?" The Church appeals every day to this proof of the divinity of its message. We do well to turn, not merely to texts of the Bible, but to the Bible itself, as the Word of God. Its body of doctrine is what may be proved out of the whole of Scripture by a reverent comparison of book with book.

Now this unity of the whole Bible is much to be noted both for argument and for personal edification. For argument, in many ways, *e.g.* Here are the books of the New Testament, with irrefragable proofs of their genuiness and authenticity. It is irrational to disjoin them from the other sections of that one great body of teaching of which they are integral parts. The lessons of spiritual life are the same, and if these lessons are the Word of God in the later books, what are we to consider them in the earlier? If these later books are both proved, by dry logical argument, to be inspired, and are also fragrant with the air of Divine truth and majesty which breathes about them, how shall we account for the old books to which they continually allude, and on which indeed they are based, being so very like them, unless they also were fashioned by the same Divine hand? Of course a Christian Father of the second century of Christianity, without any inspiration, derived the heavenly truths he taught from the inspired New Testament; but whence did Isaiah or the Psalmist learn these truths hundreds of years before the New Testament writers, unless he were taught and guided by the same God as they? I say, therefore, study the old books—drink deeply of their spirit. Note how, amid many varieties, naturally to be expected from the differences of date and the imperfection of not yet matured knowledge, they are still quite unlike heathen books, and are pervaded by the essential Gospel spirit; and you will have good reason in argument for following the Church's rule, and placing them side by side with the New Testament, and trying to understand each set of books better by the teaching of the other.

Again—still, as a matter of argument, and even leaving out of sight the proofs of the genuineness and authenticity and inspiration of the New Testament—if the various parts of the one sacred volume are thus welded together, there can be

UNITY OF THE BIBLE. 55

no rational account of the origin of the whole system, except that its beginning was from God. A man would be scouted, now-a-days, as ignorant of the first principles of historical evidence, who ventured on the monstrous assertion, that Christianity was invented by the monks of the Middle Ages. He would immediately be silenced by the question, Whence came these monks except from a pre-existing Christianity? So, with regard to the New Testament, you are in this dilemma. Either it is divine, and its divine sanction establishes the Old Testament also; or, if you hesitate as to the direct proofs of its divinity, whence came it? It stands as indissolubly united to the Old Testament as the Christianity of the Middle Ages does to that of the earlier centuries. The fact of its existence, then, implies something going before it, on which it is based, and that something (carry it back as far as you please) is so unlike the creations of mere human intelligence, that there is no rational account to be given of its origin, except that it came from God. That wonderful unity, then, which binds together the various parts in the series of the sacred books, affords very strong arguments that the whole series is from God.

But it is not for argument so much as for edification, that we value this doctrine of the unity of the Bible. Consider the lesson we thus gather as to the mode in which it ought to be studied.

The message thus delivered to us from God is one great message in many parts, to be truly understood for our life's guidance and our spiritual edification when we view it as a whole. The message is not merely a few words scattered here and there—the loved reminiscences of the Friend of our souls, with whom even in this disjointed way it would be a privilege indeed to hold intercourse. Christians, truly, store up such words, and think of them with reverence and love, as—" Come unto me, all ye that " labour and are heavy laden, and I will give " you rest."[1] " Ho! every one that thirsteth, " come ye to the waters— come ye, buy and eat, " yea, come, buy wine and milk, without money " and without price."[2] How many a soul has acknowledged the unspeakable comfort of such disjointed words. But, still, it is an inadequate view to consider even the most precious of such invitations as the whole message. Neither is the word of God confined to its commands and apophthegms—invaluable though these are as the law and guide of life. " Thou shalt love " the Lord thy God with all thy heart, with all " thy soul, with all thy mind, and with all thy " strength, and thy neighbour as thyself."[3] " Love

---

[1] Matt. xi. 28. [2] Isaiah lv. 1. [3] Luke x. 27.

UNITY OF THE BIBLE. 57

"not the world, neither the things that are in the world. If any man love the world, the love of the Father is not in him."[1] We cannot dispense with the precepts and maxims through which God thus speaks to us, and calls us to look much to the state of our hearts and our conduct day by day, and see that we are not becoming estranged from Christ. But these are not His whole message; neither is the message found only in the announcement of even those most blessed doctrines that speak of Christ's atonement. Our case would indeed be desperate, when we compared God's purity with our own sin, were it not for such announcements as—"He was wounded for our transgressions, he was bruised for our iniquities: the chastisement of our peace was upon him; and with his stripes we are healed."[2] But the message is wider in its proportions even than the doctrine of the atonement thus stated for the comfort of our separate souls. The atonement is the centre and heart of our theology; but we must not, in contemplating even the heart, overlook the well-compacted symmetry and development of the whole body.

Time would fail if, contemplating the whole Bible, we ran through its complete scheme. Note only how, in the primitive history of the Bible, God—as we Christians can understand

[1] 1 John ii. 15.   [2] Isaiah liii. 5.

Him—says to us: "All souls were created by me, and all this outward frame; the world began in me, and was loved and honoured by me before it was blighted: I have been yearning through these many centuries to win it back to myself. I created man with a free will, that he might be like myself and the blessed angels; but this very gift of a free will implied the possibility of falling, and he fell. It would have been inconsistent with my plan—it would have destroyed this free will—if I had brought him back by force, instead of winning him by love. Hence the weary history of his long estrangement. But all the various tribes throughout the world, the most degraded, have each individual man and woman of them a living soul, which I have breathed into them, and which, in spite of its degradation, mysterious as it may seem, I still love. Slaves, barbarians, savages—they are all my creatures, the subjects of my providential care. I am so near to them, though they know me not, that I mourn for their misery, and long to win them through my incarnate Son. Men have been separated into two great bands ever since the beginning—those who reject and curse, and those who listen to, my appeals. But they are all of my family, though many are rebellious, hopeless children. As long as time lasts, I shall try to win them back."

Thus God manifests himself, from the first, as the merciful Father of the human race.

Again, as the history moves on from the dark primitive ages to actual annals, God says to us: "Amid this great mass of human beings, it has ever been my way, for the benefit of the whole, to select individuals, families, nations, as the objects of my especial care and love. I have shown myself to them visibly and audibly, lest in their degradation they should lose all belief in things higher than this grovelling earth. I have taught them, I have trained them, and fenced them round with such laws and precepts as they were able to bear; ever raising them higher than their contemporaries who knew me not, even when, from the hardness of their hearts, they were not fit to receive the highest spiritual instruction, or even the highest forms of common social life. I sent them my prophets as they could bear their teaching, ever opening up the way clearer and clearer to prepare them for the coming of the Eternal Son." God Jehovah thus speaking to us, manifests himself in the tenderest way, as the Teacher, Ruler, Father, full of considerate long-suffering, preparing the way for Gospel times.

Again, God says: "In other parts of my book I give you specimens of songs of praise that you may know how the pious soul feels as to me and his own state, and how he draws near to me. I give you many examples to show how my saints walk before me, while I spare not to show you also the snares to which they are exposed and the way in which many of them fall. I tell you how I prepared the world for Christ—and how at last I sent Him. I open up to you also bright glimpses of that blessed future which awaits My faithful people at the second coming of the Son."

The time would altogether fail if we attempted even to sketch the endless variety of the whole system of divine teaching which God by his providential arrangements has thus framed from age to age, that it might tell us his whole scheme devised and accomplished for man's salvation through Jesus Christ. Note only this in closing —that thus all through the volume, if we study it as a whole indissolubly connected with the Gospel, we perceive God speaking to us in Jesus Christ, revealing himself in the most endearing relations to tribes, to families, to individuals, whatever be their circumstances and the peculiarities of their character. Whether, then, we be refined and learned or very ignorant— versed in the ways of the world or unacquainted with them like little children—whether we be high or low, in poverty and sickness, or flourishing in wealth and health—of clear intellect or bewildered by some inexplicable calamity—tempted by the devil in our weakness of character, or strong in the Holy Spirit—God in the Bible has for each of us an appropriate word of teaching in that wide-extending Gospel system which is commensurate with all our wants. No wonder that the Church jealously guards the whole book, and that good men learn more to prize every part of it, and more earnestly desire to study it, the more they know of their own deep need, and of God's mercy and goodness in Jesus Christ.

V.

THE HISTORICAL BOOKS.

[Preached at St. James's, Piccadilly.]

HEBREWS XI. 32, 33.

The time would fail me to tell of Gedeon, and of Barak, and of Samson, and of Jephthae; of David also, and Samuel, and of the prophets: Who through faith subdued kingdoms, wrought righteousness, obtained promises, stopped the mouths of lions.

MUCH of the Bible is filled with the histories of God's servants and instruments in various ages—how they were born and how they died; what they did and said in their lifetime; how with all of them the course of life was chequered, like ours, not only with happiness and calamity, but also with good deeds and bad. Maintaining the Bible to be the Word of God, we do well to look carefully at this peculiarity. The human life of the Lord Jesus and His discourses—it is natural that God should speak to us through these; the utterances of inspired prophets, foretelling and preaching; or of Apostles, commissioned under the new covenant to deliver God's message of salvation in Christ, as the prophets had their commission of old;

and the outpourings of those inspired teachers' hearts in confession, prayer, and praise—to all these we naturally listen as to the sound of a Divine voice. But ordinary history and biography, with its long roll of migrations of tribes, sieges, battles, political plots, family intrigues, hair-breadth escapes, doubtful or more than doubtful acts of violence and of cunning depicted on the same page with noble examples of self-denying patriotism and ardent faith—it requires a little more consideration to understand how God can be said to speak through these. Now, we maintain, and can prove, and have proved, that the Bible, the whole Bible, is God's appointed instrument wherein and whereby He speaks to man from age to age. Look then to this large historical portion of it—God must speak in and through it. He employed the human authors of these histories—whoever they were and whatever outward circumstances might induce them to undertake their task—for a purpose of His own, determining, by His providential arrangements, that what they wrote should serve for the edification of His Church through many centuries. Thus He has made their writings to be full of spiritual lessons; and, though I think it would be difficult, and perhaps rash, to decide —and the Church nowhere has decided—what exact amount of supernatural help He deemed it right to give or withhold from them as to the common worldly subjects which in their writings are interwoven with the Divine message, yet, in the truest sense, God speaks through them, employing them to teach great religious truths, which the world of their day either never could have known or would soon have forgotten, had they been silent. These histories and biographies, being an integral part of the Word of God, have a distinct message to us from God. We read them and prize them especially for that message, which is a spiritual message concerning religious doctrines and rules of right conduct. This message may not always be on the surface. It is our duty, and sometimes our trial, to extract it by a patient and reverent study of the narrative, as good men in the Church of God have done in all ages; and when we have gained it, and feel that we know in our understandings and consciences what God really did intend to teach us, our veneration for the Divine Voice is quite independent of any wranglings which may arise respecting the value of the human elements of the record as to extraneous matters which have nothing to do with the spiritual life or with rules of right conduct.

The man who can place himself under the divine teaching, in this intelligent and reverent spirit, finds a daily increasing satisfaction in reading these old records, which become to him, day by day, more a reality, a living voice.

It is not, however, to be denied, that even as to the spiritual and moral teaching of these books objections have been raised, which will, indeed, have no weight with Christian hearts taught of God, but which still have sometimes caused anxiety, and to which we ought to be able to give a plain and intelligent answer. Now I conceive that the catalogue of this eleventh chapter of the Epistle to the Hebrews, now before us, is of great use in this aspect. We are referred there to the history of a long list of persons, beginning with Abel and ending with Samuel, the actions of some at least of whom, as Rachab, Sampson, Jephthah, appear to us of very doubtful character. But the Epistle teaches that, whatever we may think of the individual deeds of some of them, there is a great moral in all their lives, indeed a great spiritual lesson, which lies at the root of all true religion. The ancient fathers and heroes of the Jewish race accomplished whatever they were able to achieve for their country through their belief in the unseen power and presence of God. "Faith is the substance of things hoped for, the evidence of things not seen:" And they were strong through faith. They knew that Jehovah watched over them, that their nation had a great mission

F

from Him, to maintain the pure worship of the One God, amid surrounding idolatry and polytheism; to feel His presence, and follow His guidance. It was this which nerved each weak arm for whatever great deed it could perform. It was this lively faith which distinguished the Hebrew fathers from the heroes of every other race. Wherefore, says the Apostle, in the beginning of the twelfth chapter, let us—thinking of them, and what they did, and how they did it— let us be animated by a like belief in the unseen, resist as they did, and persevere like them. We have an unseen Captain as they had to lead us. As they looked to Jehovah, let us look to Christ. "Wherefore, seeing we are compassed about with so great a cloud of witnesses, let us lay aside every weight, and the sin which doth so easily beset us, and let us run with patience the race that is set before us, looking unto Jesus the author and finisher of our faith." In their histories, even in the record of their earthly achievements, we may trace the secret of all spiritual triumphs, to keep the eye and heart ever fixed on the Lord unseen. This passage appears to me of great value, as teaching us how we are to read the history of the Old Testament, looking in each narrative it contains for some few great spiritual lessons which do in truth pervade it, and not too much distracted by such details as it must present, if it is to be set before us (as God has intended) in the continuous form of a true human history of imperfect men and women. I might illustrate this by the similar case of our Lord's parables. Each of these is intended to teach one or two simple lessons. Each has its distinct moral; and the details of the story, or of the imagery of the parable, some of which are at times even difficult to reconcile with this moral, are not to lead us away from dwelling on the great lesson or lessons, for the teaching of which the whole was designed. Each life which the Bible describes, has its point and moral like a parable; so each epoch of the history, and all the history considered as one whole. We must not be diverted to think too much of the mere adventitious circumstances which swell the narrative.

Does God, as it were, breathe through these biographies and histories? Do we feel while we read them that we are in a holy atmosphere? that the men and women, who pass before us while we read, have each their parts assigned them by God in furthering the great purpose of His will—the preparing of the world for the coming of the Lord Jesus? All Christian students taught of God feel this. When we turn from this book to any common histories, however great the deeds of which they tell, or correct the general tone of morals that pervades them, do we still feel that we have passed from a scene in which the one personal God is a living present reality, to records from which the thought of Him is excluded, or where, at the best, He is kept shrouded in the background; so that the difference between studying the word of God and any common history, is like passing from the bright noonday splendour in which the sun is felt to be shining into the shadow and gloom of some cave? And is it the one thing which our lost human nature needs to be thus enlightened and warmed by the felt presence of God? Then are we right to study these old histories by the helps which the Gospel reflects on them—to teach them continually to our children —to have their incidents so interwoven with our thoughts, that our common language and all our literature is saturated with images from their story, each of which, as it recurs to the memory, is suggestive of some good lesson. It is thus that the Church Universal has ever prized the historical books.

Shall any one tell us, that because the men whose history is thus given us by God were imperfect in their lives—and because some of them, perhaps, notwithstanding all the yearnings of God's Spirit that wooed them to His service, even made at last, so far as we can gather, a shipwreck of their faith—and because the sacred narrative, with the stern impartiality of truth, sets them before us exactly as they were with all the evil as well as all the good—that, therefore, we err in supposing that God speaks to us through the books in which He has embalmed their memory? Their sins are recorded for our warning, as their graces for our encouragement. It is the office now of the enlightened Christian conscience taught of Christ through the Holy Ghost, as it was of the conscience at all times, to discern between the good and bad in what they did and said. If with all their bright privileges their actions often show that their ideas both of morality and religion were not so pure as God of His great mercy has given to us in Jesus Christ, this is no reason why we are not to learn from them where they are fully qualified and commissioned to teach. The imperfections of the best of them—the sins of all—the melancholy fate of some amongst them whose privileges had given promise of better things—all are recorded for our learning. Their best deeds and words are to be tried by the Gospel standard: so tried they will often be found wanting. Our Lord Himself has warned us of this imperfection. "Verily I say unto you, that many prophets and righteous men have desired to see those things which ye see, and have not seen them, and to hear those things which ye hear, and have not heard them."[1]

Indeed they all stand in the same category with the Baptist. Among them that are born of women there have not risen greater: "notwithstanding he that is least in the kingdom of heaven is greater than he."[2] The stern deeds of blood, which they were often commissioned to execute, are to be judged of by the age and circumstances in which they lived, as also by the necessity of God manifesting Himself in such ages and circumstances, as a God of vengeance determined to resist and root out the abounding iniquity of the heathen. For all these things full allowance is to be made. But after all deductions this history still stands out from all human histories, proclaiming through these men's lives great spiritual truths which the heathen knew not. We say of these ancient histories, no less than of the precepts of the law, that we are wise to "have them in our hearts, to teach them diligently to our children, to tell of them when we sit in the house, and when we walk by the way, and when we lie down, and when we rise up, to write them upon the posts of our house and upon our gates."[3] As in the distinct utterances of the law and of the prophets,

[1] Matthew xiii. 17.   [2] Matthew xi. 11.
[3] Deut. vi. 7.

so in the history through His dealings with His servants from age to age, the Almighty Father proclaimed Himself of old, as He does now in Jesus Christ, to be a God of purity, of justice, and yet of mercy. It is written in Exodus (xxxiv. 6.) "The Lord passed by, and proclaimed, the Lord God, merciful and gracious, longsuffering, and abundant in goodness and truth, keeping mercy for thousands, forgiving iniquity, transgression, and sin, and that will by no means clear the guilty."

To sum up. It is quite true that, dissevered from the Gospel, these historical books of the Old Testament, with all their excellences, would teach an imperfect system. Of course without the New Testament they would teach Judaism, which, in its very nature, is granted to be imperfect, and not the doctrine and law of Christ. We, as disciples of the Lord Jesus, have the foundation of our faith in Him. But casting our glance back on the old records, lighted up by His and the apostles' commentary, and taking His rules as our guide in their interpretation, we find abundant help and comfort in them all. It is thus, by His aid, that we read them for our edification and teach them to our children. Looking to Him as the author and finisher of our own more perfect faith—our guide in life and support in death— we find even in the most common passages of this old history continual lessons which God caused to be written, not only to give to the men of the old times such instruction as they could bear in their generation, but to edify Christ's people in the bright gospel times.

VI.

THE BIBLE INFLUENCING THE CHRISTIAN LIFE.

[Preached at St. James's, Piccadilly.]

COLOSSIANS III. 16.

Let the word of Christ dwell in you richly in all wisdom; teaching and admonishing one another in psalms and hymns and spiritual songs, singing with grace in your hearts to the Lord.

GOD has given us His word that it may influence our whole lives. "Let the word of Christ dwell in you." I do not understand the word of Christ to express exactly the idea which we denote by the word of God. Yet the word of Christ must here mean nearly this—the teaching of God, in and through Christ. And for us Christians—who have in our hands the life of Christ and His discourses, and the scheme of doctrine and of practical precept unfolded by His apostles, and who know how all the Old Testament has been incorporated by Him into His system, and how, when rightly understood, it is all full of Him, and how the depths of its meaning in its various parts are only truly apprehended when we read it by the light He has shed on it—for us Christians, the whole Bible becomes the word of Christ in virtue of its being the word of God. The Church has ever so regarded it—good men in the Church have ever so used it.

Let the word of Christ dwell in you richly. The Apostle seems to say, Let the Gospel, the teaching of Christ, explained and brought home to your hearts by the Spirit of Christ, let the word of Christ, or the word of God, dwell in you richly; you will thus be taught all wisdom, and be enabled to teach others wisely.

In that first age, in which this Epistle was written, the word of Christ might still refer to lively revelations of the will of God in Christ, made directly to the hearts of the inspired, as well as to the written record of such revelation. For us now God speaks through a written record, which is, for us, the word of Christ. The lesson before us is—master the spirit of this record in its fulness—let the word of Christ dwell in you richly—let it dictate your principles of action. Turn your thoughts continually to the images of God's fatherly relation to you which the word of God sets forth—images so full of love that by them the feelings are stirred to love Him in return, and to hate sin, and thus the will is led where the reason guides. Make yourselves so familiar with this word that, even when you cease to look at the letter of its teaching, its spirit shall breathe through all you say and think, so that, whether in private or in the assemblies of the Church, whether you are praising God by singing hymns, or speaking for each other's edification, a holy atmosphere, wafted from the word of God in Christ, shall be diffused all around. "Let the word of Christ dwell in you richly in all wisdom, teaching and admonishing one another in Psalms and Hymns and Spiritual Songs, singing with grace in your hearts to the Lord."

The testimony of all good men shows that they who would live a really Christian life, guided by the Spirit and word of Christ, have need habitually to refresh themselves by the study of the Bible; and that the sort of study which is needed is more or less devotional. This is enforced on us by the order of the Church: why otherwise should it be set before us as a rule that so large a portion of the Bible is to be read every day, and why should this reading be incorporated with our forms of worship unless with the view of showing us what is the proper attitude and frame of mind in which to read? The scholar is in his proper place, studying the sacred records with his apparatus of criticism, and all the helps of philology, geography, and history. He who would unfold and illustrate the principles of taste can never succeed, unless he is familiar with these sacred specimens of poetry and of history. The common historian and the philosopher must seek here continually for illustrations of what human nature is, and what are the phases through which it has passed since the globe was first peopled. And each of these incidentally, as he follows his own pursuit, will be of great use in throwing light on the principles by which we are to interpret God's word and ascertain with accuracy its real meaning. But, the meaning once ascertained, each of these men, when he puts aside his professional avocation, and considers simply what is good for the life of his own soul, is taught that he must read as a child reads, not to judge but to be guided—determined to drink in the pure lessons which spring abundantly from the living fountain. Our children are taught to repeat the Advent Collect before they read the Bible. And every real Christian feels that He, who has caused all Holy Scripture to be written for our learning, must guide and control our thoughts by his blessed Spirit, if, as He has intended, through the study of His word we are to have our whole life and conduct and modes of feeling, speaking, judging, leavened by His teaching.

Truly, my friends, in this busy London life of ours, so full of laborious idleness for the gay, as well as of distracting labour for the thoughtful, the freshness of our faith must wither, and our good thoughts of God, and Christ, and eternity, must be all dissipated by cares of earth, if we do not make a marked pause every day, to refresh ourselves by re-perusing or thinking over some portion of the message which God has sent to us from heaven. It would be wise to take care that our morning reading shall always leave in our memory some terse saying or vividly described example, the thought of which may help us against temptation throughout the day.

Who knows not the wonderful force with which texts have made the power of Him whose utterances they are, felt in the history of souls, the sound of truths not loved, but still believed, ringing shrill, in spite of all efforts to silence them, in unwilling ears? "What shall it profit a man, if he gain the whole world and lose his own soul?"[1] We know how this question tormented, and at last subdued, the destined missionary, while, hurrying through scenes of intoxicating pleasure, he sought refuge from an awakening conscience in the adulation which everywhere greeted his popularity, as he entered each crowded assembly. The Christians of the early days were not unwise in seeking to embody spiritual lessons from the Bible in their works of art: that the sculptured figure, *e.g.* of the Good Shepherd, casually seen, might call back his wandering sheep; or the ark, floating over the waste of waters, speak of the only escape from the deluge

[1] Mark viii. 36.

of God's wrath; or the Good Samaritan, binding up the wounds which violent men had inflicted, speak of a Friend ever near to soothe and heal the broken heart while the world passes by unheeding. The adornments of our own churches, memorials of this sacred teaching, are felt by all of us not to be useless for winning the heart to holy thought. Our fathers of the puritan time, afraid of the old symbolism, still did not discard a like help—the inscription over the doorway, marking to whom those who planned it looked for a blessing on their work—"unless the Lord build the house their labour is but lost that build it;"[1] the bed-chamber with its oak-panels emblazoned, "I will lay me down in peace and sleep, for thou, Lord, only makest me to dwell in safety;"[2] or "He giveth his beloved sleep;"[3] or the ceiling of the Hall of Entertainment, preaching from the 145th Psalm, "The eyes of all wait upon Thee, and thou givest them their meat in due season."[4] Who does not recognise in all these a calm, reverential sense of our dependence on the teaching of God's word, and a desire to fulfil Moses's injunction, that His precepts may be always present to our eyes, and thus sink into our hearts[5]— a desire, indeed, that the word of Christ may

---

[1] Psalm cxxvii. 1.   [2] Psalm iv. 8.   [3] Psalm cxxvii. 2.
[4] Psalm cxlv. 15.   [5] Deut. vi. 7.

dwell amongst us, and in us abundantly—the same desire which dictated the reading of some grave godly lesson from the lectern by the dais in the halls of old monasteries, that the thought of Christ's word might check irreverent mirth? All these customs may degenerate into formalism; but they testify, in their origin, to the longing of earnest Christians, in all ages and of all schools of opinion, to assign its due influence to the word of God as the regulator of our whole lives—an influence which has never been assigned to the words of mere human teachers. If Solomon could say of the instruction of good earthly parents,—" My son, keep thy father's commandment, and forsake not the law of thy mother: Bind them continually upon thine heart, and tie them about thy neck. When thou goest, it shall lead thee; when thou sleepest, it shall keep thee; and when thou awakest, it shall talk with thee,"[1]—Christians have felt that this can only be true of the counsels of human friends in so far as they are based on the word of God—that it is only of God's word, explained in Christ, that we can say with perfect fulness of meaning, "The commandment is a lamp and the law is light, and reproofs of instruction are the way of life."[2] For "the law of the Lord"— and it only—"is perfect, converting the soul;

[1] Prov. vi. 20—22.   [2] Ibid. ver. 23.

the testimony of the Lord is sure, making wise the simple; the statutes of the Lord are right, rejoicing the heart; the commandment of the Lord is pure, enlightening the eyes."[1]

It would be satisfactory to know into how many gatherings of the wealthy and gay the thought of the lessons of God's word finds ready admission. Doubtless in the crowds assembled on great occasions of festivity, into which it is quite possible to enter without any undue dissipation of the thoughts or any concentration of the desires on objects purely worldly, there are always many who, entering merely because their position seems to require it, and because they find therein an innocent relaxation, have no difficulty in recalling at any moment the thought of God's teaching as their guide while they are moving in such scenes. But it cannot be doubted there are many others for whom the world has become a god—who, mingling in such scenes, give themselves up to them—cannot live without them, and naturally and truly feel that there is an incongruity between their passionate pursuit of pleasure as an end, and any reverential obedience to the word of God.

Let all then who live in the world, if they would be safe, put to themselves this question

---

[1] Psalm xix. 7, 8.

often and seriously, Have I any difficulty in recalling the thought of the Lord Jesus Christ's warning voice in the scenes in which I am moving? In the way in which I enter on such scenes is there anything inconsistent with the holy precepts and example of the Lord who died for me? Is there any reason why I should be more startled in this society than in any other, if the intelligence were suddenly announced that at this moment the Lord was calling me to deliver up my soul? Such questions seriously asked and honestly answered will enable us to see whether or no we are forgetting the word of Christ from the hubbub of human voices in the world around us. Certainly no society is safe for us, in which we have a difficulty in recalling and acting on the word of Christ. This word is given by God to be with us at all times, to be the regulator of our whole lives. We see in this how different it is from the words of mere human teachers.

Again, Am I here in a world full of sickness and sorrow? When I lie down at night, though all things are going well with me and mine, it is still, from the necessary condition of our humanity, quite uncertain how we shall fare on the morrow. Some inevitable blow may in the night fall upon us or those dearest to us. My friends, think of your past lives and their sudden reverses; or, if your own life's tenor has been even, think of your neighbour's fate. In those great emergencies of life, which come so suddenly and are so overwhelming, it is marvellous how comforting for Christ's people is the force of texts darting into the memory. "I the Lord thy God will hold thy right hand, saying unto thee, Fear not; I will help thee."[1] "Though he slay me, yet will I trust in him."[2] "Yea, though I walk through the valley of the shadow of death, I will fear no evil: thy rod and thy staff they comfort me."[3]

These Old Testament assurances, quickened by a power from Christ, are as fresh and powerful for comfort as the words which flowed from His own gracious lips. So wonderfully is the word of God distinguished from mere human words by the quickening power which Christ gives it.

The Church, then, and the Apostle urge you to study the word of God, for your soul's refreshment, as you study no other words. And we may be contented to rest the whole on this further claim to your attention. Consider how many death-beds, otherwise hopeless, have been comforted and sustained, and made full of hope,

[1] Isaiah xli. 3.   [2] Job xiii. 15.   [3] Psalm xxiii. 4.

by the thought that Christ was speaking to the dying, through some remembrance of His Word. The death-bed of a good heathen, summoning up all his natural courage and thinking of all human sources of consolation, is worthy to be admired: but even in the most cultivated heathen times we find few of such examples, and even in the best of them there is a felt blank. But not a week passes in Christian times in which some dying sufferer, with or without any natural advantages or refined training, is not marvellously sustained in the last emergency by hearing Christ speak to him through familiar texts, or through hymns which are but amplifications of texts. Speaking to themselves in psalms and hymns and spiritual songs, such sufferers feel their trials all lightened, if not removed, by having the word of Christ dwelling in them. It is a great privilege which we Christians enjoy, that not for increase in knowledge only or growth in civilization and refinement, but for our actual support in difficulties which would otherwise overwhelm us, we have here a store of words of ancient wisdom through which the living Christ speaks to us and sustains our souls. The thought of what the Bible is to us at such seasons is the best antidote against any irreverent treatment of it, against any study of it which does not recognize it as different from all other books, and receive its lessons not as what man's wisdom teacheth, but what the Holy Ghost teacheth.

THE END.

M. CLAY, SON, AND TAYLOR, PRINTERS, BREAD STREET HILL.

www.ingramcontent.com/pod-product-compliance
Lightning Source LLC
Chambersburg PA
CBHW020302090426
42735CB00009B/1189